Loving Your Work

The Lessons Learned Series

Learn how the most accomplished leaders from around the globe have tackled their toughest challenges in the Harvard Business Press *Lessons Learned* series.

Concise and engaging, each volume in this series offers fourteen insightful essays by top leaders in industry, the public sector, and academia on the most pressing issues they've faced. The *Lessons Learned* series also offers all of the lessons in their original video format, free bonus videos, and other exclusive features on the 50 Lessons companion Web site: **www.50lessons.com/work**.

Both in print and online, *Lessons Learned* contributors share surprisingly personal and insightful anecdotes and offer authoritative and practical advice drawn from their years of hard-won experience.

A crucial resource for today's busy executive, *Lessons Learned* gives you instant access to the wisdom and expertise of the world's most talented leaders.

Other books in the series:

Leading by Example

Managing Change

Managing Your Career

Managing Conflict

Starting a Business

Hiring and Firing

Making the Sale

Executing for Results

Sparking Innovation

Making Strategy Work

Doing Business Globally

Going Green

Weathering the Storm

Crisis as Opportunity

Motivating People

Overcoming Obstacles

Communicating Clearly

Unleashing Talent

Doing Business Ethically

Loving Your Work

LES50NS

www.50lessons.com/work

Boston, Massachusetts

Printed in the United States of America
14 13 12 11 10   5 4 3 2 1

No part of this publication may be reproduced, stored
in or introduced into a retrieval system, or transmitted,
in any form, or by any means (electronic, mechanical,
photocopying, recording, or otherwise), without the
prior permission of the publisher. Requests for
permission should be directed to permissions@hbsp.
harvard.edu, or mailed to Permissions, Harvard Business
School Publishing, 60 Harvard Way, Boston,
Massachusetts 02163.

Library of Congress Cataloging-in-Publication Data

Loving your work.
     p. cm. — (Lessons learned)
   ISBN 978-1-4221-3986-8 (pbk. : alk. paper)
  1.   Job satisfaction. 2.   Career development.
3.   Career changes. 4.   Quality of work life.
I.   Fifty Lessons (Firm)
   HF5549.5.J63L68 2009
   650.1—dc22

                              2009036017

⇥ A NOTE FROM THE ⇤
PUBLISHER

In partnership with 50 Lessons, a leading
provider of digital media content, Harvard
Business Press is pleased to offer *Lessons
Learned*, a book series that showcases the
trusted voices of the world's most experi-
enced leaders. Through the power of personal storytelling, each book in this series
presents the accumulated wisdom of some
of the world's best-known experts and offers
insights into how these individuals think,
approach new challenges, and use hard-won
lessons from experience to shape their leadership philosophies. Organized thematically
according to the topics at the top of managers' agendas—leadership, change management, entrepreneurship, innovation, and
strategy, to name a few—each book draws
from 50 Lessons' extensive video library
of interviews with CEOs and other thought
leaders. Here, the world's leading senior

A Note from the Publisher

executives, academics, and business thinkers speak directly and candidly about their triumphs and defeats. Taken together, these powerful stories offer the advice you'll need to take on tomorrow's challenges.

As you read this book, we encourage you to visit **www.50lessons.com/work** to view videos of these lessons as well as additional bonus material on this topic. You'll find not only new ways of looking at the world, but also the tried-and-true advice you need to illuminate the path forward.

⊰ CONTENTS ⊱

1. Warren Bennis
   Love What You Do   1

2. Maxine Clark
   **The Retail Experience
   Should Be Fun**   7

3. Howard Lester
   Do What You Love   15

4. Jerry Rice
   Living the Dream   19

5. Stacy Peralta
   Do Your Own Thing   23

6. Amy Butte
   Forging Your Own Career Path   27

7. Peter Seligmann
   **The Power of Personal
   Conviction**   33

Contents

8. Erroll Davis Jr.
   **Creating the Appropriate
   Work-Life Balance**   41

9. Laura Tyson
   Keeping Your Balance   47

10. Peggy Fleming
    Strive for Perfection   55

11. William Harrison
    **Step Out of Your
    Comfort Zone**   59

12. Kay Koplovitz
    **Always Be on the Lookout
    for Big Ideas**   65

13. Cali Ressler and Jody Thompson
    **Focus on Retaining Talent,
    Not Hiring**   71

14. Sir David Bell
    The Way We Work   79

    About the Contributors   85
    Acknowledgments   99

Loving Your Work

Love What You Do

Warren Bennis

Distinguished Professor of Business Administration
Marshall School of Business, University
of Southern California

I ACCEPTED A job as provost at State University of New York at Buffalo. No one could understand why I would leave a tenured position in a corner office at MIT, overlooking the gorgeous Charles River, and go to Buffalo, New York. I had just seen a play, *A Chorus Line*, in New York, and there's

Loving Your Work

a line from that play which goes, "To com-
mit suicide in Buffalo is redundant." Then,
I went off to Buffalo to become a provost, to
become a first-time administrator, hoping
I would then become university president.
Four years later I did, when I became presi-
dent of the University of Cincinnati where
I was for seven years.

A key event occurred in my next-to-last
year as president of the University of
Cincinnati. I was asked by somebody at
Harvard, who was then dean of the School
of Education—a remarkable human being
named Paul Ylvisaker—if I would come to
the School of Ed and give a talk on leading a
contemporary university. I really poured my
heart into that talk. It was 1977. It was in
Longfellow Hall in the School of Ed. It
looked like a bit of a small law school room,
very subtly tiered, about a hundred and
twenty-five people, mainly faculty and grad-
uate students.

I was talking about leading a contemporary university. I had that sense that the
speech was really going well, that sense one

feels when they think they're at the top of their game and they're just connecting with the audience, as I felt I was. Then there was Q&A, and I felt again that I was handling this group with great adroitness and skill, and they were responding in a way that gave me more energy. All of us who've given speeches know what it's like to really feel that you're even better than you usually are. That's what I felt.

Then Paul Ylvisaker, who was sitting at the very back of that small auditorium, lobbed a question to me. You could almost see the scene; it was like a softball, with the seam slowly coming. The question came over the heads of everybody in that audience, and it was like a shot to the gut. I was not stumped but totally upended and speechless with this question, which was unexpected. I don't know how long I stood in helpless silence. I'm sure not for more than five seconds, but I could actually hear my heart beating. I finally looked up. I forget what look I must have had, but probably a helpless look.

Loving Your Work

I just said, "Paul, I don't know. I don't know."

Because his question was, "Do you love being president? Do you love being president of the University of Cincinnati?"

That's what I said, "I don't know" to, and I never recovered my rhythm. Thankfully, he ended it, said thank you, allowed one more question, and that was it.

On the plane back to Cincinnati the next morning, I did know the answer to that question: I didn't want to do that.

It's interesting, and it's another whole story about what he was picking up. What was he picking up? I only can guess, because Paul Ylvisaker had diabetes, which I didn't know at the time. Before I could phone him to say, "Paul, what in the world led you to ask that? What were you seeing in my eyes?" he'd passed away.

I really believe that I wanted to *be* a university president more than I wanted to *do* it; there were a lot of things about it that I didn't really love. Every interaction I had was transactional. Every interaction

Love What You Do

I had was, how much can I get? How much do you want? So what it taught me was, if you don't really love what you're doing, I don't think you can be happy at it. I don't think you can be good at it over the long haul.

And the minute you stop loving it—and I don't mean every day; I don't mean you're dying to get up every day to go to work; that's ridiculous—but how else can you pull from others? How can you give meaning to what you're doing and to others? How can you contage [sic] your passion if you don't have it? You can't put it on.

So I realized that if you want to be a good leader—a good leader, just good—you've got to really love it. You've got to love it.

TAKEAWAYS

⚑ If you don't love what you're doing, you won't be happy at it or good at it over the long haul.

Loving Your Work

‡ If you don't love what you do, how can you give meaning to it or to others you're working with?

———◆———

The Retail Experience Should Be Fun

———◆———

Maxine Clark

Chief Executive Bear, Build-A-Bear

THIS STORY STARTS long before Build-A-Bear Workshop ever came to be. Little did I know what was brewing in the back of my own heart and head. Maybe it started when I was ten years old and I lost my teddy bear. I always loved that teddy bear, and I still was looking for him every day.

Probably my biggest inspiration came from Stanley Goodman, who was the chairman of the May Company when I joined as an executive trainee in 1972. Stanley said to a group of young, ambitious buyers and assistant buyers that retailing is entertainment and the store is a stage. When the customers have fun, they spend more money. That made a lot of sense to me, because I loved to shop. When I was shopping and buying things that were adding to my life, it really did make me happy, so it clicked. It was that moment that I said, "This is what I'm supposed to do. This is my calling."

Everything I did from that point forward, whether I was a hosiery or sportswear buyer, or a shoe merchandise manager, was about how to make it more fun for the customer. The other side, too, was that I was the ultimate customer, maybe not always being able to afford to buy certain things but observing, seeing, and knowing what the customer wanted. Quite frankly, it bothered me that people didn't seem to be more interested in my experience as a consumer.

"What do you want? What are we missing? What would you like to have in our store?"

All these things were building up in me as I went through my retail career, moving from an executive trainee to, ultimately, the president of Payless ShoeSource, which was a very large and wonderful company.

But all this time, I'm thinking that business needs to be fun. Remember what Stanley said about fun? In 1996, I was working on a big project for the shoe business, and I thought, "Where's the fun? What does the customer really want?" I started talking to customers, not about a teddy bear business, but about the shoe business.

Mothers would say to me, "Why does Payless do it this way; why can't you do it that way? Why can't the shoes be more comfortable?"

It dawned on me that there was more out there. We really need to get to the customers. I decided that the creativity of the

business was missing for me. I needed to go
and do something on my own. I didn't know
exactly what that was going to be, but I did
know for sure it was going to be for children, because children require you to be
creative on an ongoing basis.

I remember as a child going window
shopping with my mother. We couldn't
really afford to buy much, but looking in
the windows was an experience. Imagine
that. The windows were so imaginative and
creative that you could spend fifteen minutes staring at the window of a department
store and not see everything that there was
to buy. You'd go into a department store,
and they'd have a fashion show in the tea
room or out on the floor, or they'd have a
sampling in the housewares department.
Those types of things were actually missing
from the business. I felt that when I was a
child and I would go to those experiences,
it could be fun. Why did you have to go
to Disney World to have a good time?
Why couldn't you have a good time at
the mall? What had happened to that

experience that Stanley talked about, that when the customers have fun they spend more money?

I think retailers forgot what the experience really means. It's not just about paying at the cash register. It's about the minute you walk into that mall or drive into the parking garage: What does it feel like? Is it easy to find a place to park? Is it well lit? All those things contribute, especially to a female consumer, a mom, and what she's viewing as part of her experience. It is so much more than whether people are nice and what products you're buying.

We forgot about that. The fun went out of the business, and as retailers we started to take ourselves far too seriously. We were so worried about price, the deal, and how big we could get. We could blame it on Wall Street or we could blame it on real estate developers and how many malls there were, but the blame rested with all of us. We forgot what the customer wanted because we forgot to talk to them. We forgot to ask them.

Loving Your Work

At the beginning of the twenty-first century, we have all these tools—the Internet—for consumers to communicate with us. They can tell us what they like; we can find out information. How are we going to use it to create a new form of specialty retailing? I think we've done that at Build-A-Bear Workshop. So much of it is old-fashioned—talking to the customer, spending a lot of time in the stores, working with them, and being excited about each new opening. It's the way we talk to customers using all the technological tools that we can to make communication easy and more targeted.

TAKEAWAYS

⊰ For customers, the retail experience encompasses much more than the salespeople they encounter and the products they buy.

The Retail Experience

🗝 Retailers today have technological tools that make targeted communication with customers easy.

🗝 When customers have fun, they spend more money.

Do What You Love

Howard Lester

Chairman and CEO, Williams–Sonoma

I GOT INTO this business in the summer of 1978, and it was kind of an interesting period in my life. I'd grown up in the computer services and software business, had finally sold the company, and was living in Southern California and loafing; really playing golf. I started feeling like a degenerate. I was only in my early forties and just didn't have anything to do. All of my friends were working, so I couldn't even find anybody to have lunch with.

I started thinking a lot about what I wanted to do and what was going to make me happy, and I realized that to that point in my working career, I had kind of done the things that were necessary. I was trying to make a living and just do the best I could and make money, but I was never really happy. I wasn't excited about getting out of bed in the morning and going to work, so I gave a lot of thought to what it was that I wanted to do, and I knew it was something different.

One of the main conclusions that I reached was that it was important for me at that point in my life—as I mentioned, I was in my early forties—to do something. You know, "This is not a dress rehearsal." I wanted to do things that I loved doing. Why go through life doing things that you don't love doing? I felt that if I was doing something I loved, I'd have a better chance of being good at it than doing something

Do What You Love

I didn't love, because it wouldn't be work. It would be joy.

So I went on a little journey of looking at a lot of businesses, some of them pretty weird. And one day I came across this little company called Williams-Sonoma, which was struggling. It was a little, U.S., $4 million company with four stores and a small catalog, located in San Francisco. One thing led to another, and I was able to purchase the business in the summer of 1978.

We've been very fortunate. We've grown a business that we're quite proud of, and I can tell you that over the last twenty-seven years, I don't think there's been a day or a morning where I wasn't excited about getting up and going to work. I've loved what we do, I've loved our customers, and I've loved our merchandise.

I'm so proud of what we do. Every time I walk into a store or pick up a catalog or look on the Internet, I'm just so proud of our people and what our customers say about us. It's been a wonderful experience for me.

TAKEAWAYS

- ⚞ Life is not a dress rehearsal, so it's important to give thought and devote time to finding work you can commit to with passion and pride.

- ⚞ Doing things you love doesn't feel like work; it feels like joy and increases your chance of success.

———◆◆◆———

Living the Dream

———◆◆◆———

Jerry Rice

Three-Time Super Bowl Champion;
Former Wide Receiver, San Francisco 49ers

I USED TO run unpaved roads. I didn't know why I was running. Then it happened. It all came into focus, and I knew the reason why I was the way I was, the reason why I was training so hard and exerting so much energy. I was meant to be a professional football player: someone who goes out there, entertains people, and brings so much excitement to their lives. That was something I always wanted to do, and I think I have gotten everything out of football.

If someone had told me I was destined to be a professional football player way back in the day, I would have thought they were crazy. When I was running, it was always one hundred degrees out there. It was funny because my mom would look at me and say, "Son, why are you torturing yourself this way?" Who would've known that I was going to have the opportunity to play with some Hall of Famers, or one of the best coaches, Bill Walsh, or owner Eddie DeBartolo? I was preparing myself.

It taught me that you never know what you're destined for. But when the time is right, you had better be ready. I took advantage of my opportunity. That's why I still have to pinch myself.

I've had the opportunity to live a dream, to do so much and touch so many lives—on the football field, and off the football field with *Dancing with the Stars*. I was able to reach a whole different demographic that was not into sports. "This guy, he's a professional football player, and now he's trying to dance." Everybody thought at first, "Why is he doing this to himself?"

I knew nothing about ballroom dancing or any other type of dancing. I felt like it would be a challenge. I have five-year-old little kids who don't know anything about me from football, but they know about me from *Dancing with the Stars*.

It was about stepping out on that edge and saying to myself, "Look, yeah, I'm going to take a chance."

Many people would love to do that, but they're afraid to. They don't want to step out of their element and take a chance. I was willing to do that.

TAKEAWAYS

⚑ You never know what you're destined for, but when the time is right, be ready to take advantage of your opportunity.

Loving Your Work

⚐ If you don't let fear stop you from
stepping out of your element and
taking a chance, you may find success,
as well as increased opportunities.

Do Your
Own Thing

Stacy Peralta

Former Professional Skateboarder;
Director, Dogtown and Z-Boys

I KNOW A couple of friends right now who want to transition into something else. The one thing they always say is, "I'm scared to do it."

The thing is, you *are* scared to do it. You're *going* to be scared to do it, and you are never *not* going to be scared to do it. The whole point is you've got to embrace the insecurity and the fear factor. There is no easy way out of this, but if you go into it knowing that, it'll make it easier. Instead of, for instance, thinking, "I must get rid of this insecurity; I must get rid of this fear," just say, "I'll learn to live with it, but I'm still going to go with what I want to do."

When I started succeeding making my skateboarding videos, I started getting work in Hollywood because many producers in Hollywood were noticing that their children were watching my skateboarding videos. They started watching them and liked what I was doing. So I started getting opportunities to work in television as a director.

At first, it was fun; I enjoyed it. After about a year or two, I found out that I wasn't enjoying it at all and that I was stuck. For the first time in my life, I felt that I was punching in and punching out. For the first time in my life, I really felt, "Wow, I'm on the job. I have a job to go to."

It was no longer fun anymore. It was at that point where I realized, "I don't want to do this. I can't do this. I'm not getting any fulfillment out of this. What can I do?"

What I did is I looked back on my life and I thought, "What have I succeeded at in my life before?"

I've always succeeded when I did my own thing.

It was at that point where I started cooking up the idea for my own film. That film was my first documentary, *Dogtown and Z-Boys*, which we got Vans, the shoe company, to finance. That was the film that enabled me to transition out of television and into the documentary film world. It would have never happened had I not gone through that unhappiness and realization that I wasn't getting what I needed in television. The money was good; I could have done it for life, but it just wasn't bringing happiness. I wanted to do something else.

TAKEAWAYS

- ⚔ Some fear and insecurity are inevitable in making the transition to a new line of work.

- ⚔ Instead of thinking you must get rid of insecurity and fear, determine to live with them and do what you want to do in spite of them.

- ⚔ Unhappiness can be a necessary impetus to seeking work that is more fulfilling.

Forging Your Own Career Path

Amy Butte

Former Chief Financial Officer,
MF Group

THE QUESTION IS, what is the greatest challenge that I have faced in my career? Ironically, the greatest challenge happened in my first job right out of school. I left Yale and joined Andersen Consulting in their change management practice. I say "ironically," because so much of my life today is about change.

I said, "Oh, this is great. I'll get to be a consultant and learn about technology, change, and organizations."

And instead of learning about all of that, I showed up my first day, and there was no work in change management. So there I was, a people person learning how to code in COBOL. Well, I really was a square peg in a round hole, and the challenge for me was not just in the tasks that I was asked to do but also the environment, which was very much a wait-your-turn type of environment. What I realized very quickly is, I'm not a wait-your-turn type of person; that just because I didn't have the seniority didn't mean I didn't think that I could do something. It was a very uncomfortable situation.

The challenge was, "Where do I go next?" And I said to myself, "What type of environment do I want to be in?" I wanted to be in a meritocracy. "What type of work do I want to do, or where do I want to be?"

Forging Your Own Career Path

I love New York. I didn't want to leave New York. The best place to be if you want to be in New York City really is Wall Street, so I set a path to Wall Street.

It was really about stepping back. Here I was, coming out of college with a political science and psychology degree, yet I was being branded as either an accountant or a technologist, and I was neither an accountant nor a technologist. So I had kind of lost my chance at some of the management training programs. It was an off time of year, and I really had to find a software development company—somebody who serviced Wall Street, people who provided information, knowledge—and learn how to be an expert in terms of servicing people on the Street.

So I networked. I talked to people, asked their advice, talked to headhunters, and found my way to a small software development company that was basically developing the early-stage order management systems, or trading systems. It was the first time LAN technology was being used on trading desks and with portfolio managers. And it was really through that company that I learned what Wall Street was. What's the difference between an upstairs trader and a downstairs trader? What's the difference between the buy side and the sell side? What's the difference between back office and front office? It was really being a part of that company and interacting with my clients that I learned a lot and started on that path to Wall Street.

The lesson to be learned from this challenge is to set a path, and even if your direction shifts, it's OK. You can still get somewhere. But be clear about where you want to go. You can always change your mind, but it's important to be focused in one direction or another. Even though it took me from being a management consultant to working for a software development company, to working for an information system company, to business school, to being a research analyst, to the New York Stock Exchange, it was all about the path of getting closer and closer to being a part of Wall Street.

I think the second lesson that I would take from it is that if you don't feel right in an organization, there is probably a reason for it. There are plenty of people who can feel like a square peg in a round hole, but it's important to make sure that you find that fit for yourself.

I think the third lesson that I would probably try to give people is that you're going to suffer disappointments in your career. It's really easy to take that time, right after a disappointment, and want to hide, not want to get up. And it's especially hard for people who've been successful in their lives and in their careers to get up and try to do it again, but you will overcome those disappointments. They'll make you stronger.

TAKEAWAYS

- ᛤ Set a path, and even if your direction shifts, it's OK because you can still get somewhere if you're clear about where you want to go.

- ᛤ Take responsibility to find the right fit in the right organization for yourself.

- ᛤ Accept that you're going to suffer disappointments in your career, but also realize that you will overcome them and they'll make you stronger.

The Power of Personal Conviction

Peter Seligmann

*Cofounder, Chairman, and CEO,
Conservation International*

IN 1986, I was working for the Nature
Conservancy, and I took a sabbatical. I went
to Costa Rica and then to Peru with my
family. I was struck by the juxtaposition and

the contrast between the spectacular natural richness and the poverty of people. I came back and advocated to colleagues of mine at the Nature Conservancy that we needed to focus on human well-being in working on conservation efforts internationally.

I was also supportive of my friends who were working in international conservation at the Nature Conservancy in that so much of biological diversity globally is outside of the United States, yet so much of what the Nature Conservancy was doing was inside the United States. I really felt we needed to shift the focus of our efforts in terms of *where* we were working, but also, instead of acquiring land—which was what the Nature Conservancy was doing—we should be thinking about how you engage people so that they benefit from conservation, so that they address their poverty issues.

Over a period of months, I switched from my job at the Nature Conservancy in California to running the international program of the Nature Conservancy. I was asking them to look at how they were doing science, how they engaged with communities, how they made their priorities, and to shift financial resources from the United States to overseas. This created a lot of stress. It culminated in a request by the leadership of the Nature Conservancy for me to just deal with business as usual: acquire land around the world. I said it wouldn't work because we didn't own it.

For conservation to work in another country, you have to build the capacity in that country. It has to be owned by locals. We can't control it. For it to survive, for conservation efforts to last for a long time, people have to make money. You can't tell a poor person, "Don't cut a forest." They might feel guilty, but they're going to do what they have to do to live. I was basically told to cease and desist with what I was doing. I knew that that was wrong, and I knew that we had the right strategy and we needed to pursue it.

It was in January 1987—when I was given this order by the Nature Conservancy that we had to stick to the knitting of the

organization—that I contacted the leadership in the organization, the board members, and said that we had a real crisis
because we knew it wouldn't work and we
didn't believe that it was the right approach
to dealing with environmental issues outside
the United States. The end result was that
the board members who were participating
called me up and said, "We've resolved all
the problems."

And I said to them, "Well, I'm glad you
resolved the problems, but while you were
in the meeting, I got fired."

When I went back to my hotel room in
Washington, D.C., at the Tabard Inn, all
the people who worked for me in the international program, all the people we'd hired
who were from other countries—from
Mexico, Costa Rica, Peru, and Bolivia—had
gathered in my hotel room. They had
signed a letter saying that if I left, they
wanted to continue the approach we'd had
or they would resign.

That night, in late January 1987, 85 per-
cent of the international program of the

Personal Conviction

Nature Conservancy decided to start a new organization with these different principles, which were focusing on creating a new science that would work for biodiversity efforts outside of the United States, focusing on economic well-being. We incorporated the organization the next day. Basically, we were homeless and penniless, but we had started Conservation International.

That's when I learned the power of personal conviction; that if you stick to what you believe in and you follow what is true and right, it will resonate with people who have similar beliefs. When you have that coherence of idea and philosophy, that's how you can accomplish great things. You've gotten down to where you can't be pushed down or cracked, because you really believe in something.

What was fascinating was that we went out in the next couple of days and talked to some individuals, and within a week, we had $3 million to support this group of people, from individuals who said, "We really believe in what you're doing." So it was, basically, a few beliefs that were held to be true that allowed us to begin to build an organization. Those core beliefs are still the belief system of Conservation International. And we've grown. We've grown from a small band of thirty or forty people to a group with twelve hundred employees around the world and a budget of about $140 million.

But the core values are values that we held true to ourselves, and they're values that we use now as we hire people, when we look for partners, when we engage people. It's talking to everybody around the world about what's in your heart, not just what's in your mind, and how you link those together to value an environment that's so important for our children and our future.

TAKEAWAYS

- If you stick to what you believe in and follow what is true and right, the power of personal conviction will resonate with people who have similar beliefs.

- To value an environment that's important for children and for the future, you have to link what's in your mind with what's in your heart.

———◆◆◆———

Creating the Appropriate Work-Life Balance

———◆◆◆———

Erroll Davis Jr.

Former Chairman, Alliant Energy Corporation

ONE OF THE great challenges I had as a CEO was creating the appropriate work-life balance. It's never easy, particularly for ambitious people working their way up, to appropriately balance their work life with their family life, their friends, and building relationships, things of that nature. I think I'm as guilty as most senior executives. I certainly tried, and it's extremely difficult.

When my daughter was in junior high school, I coached the eighth grade girls' basketball team. I would leave work at 3:00 p.m. in the afternoon, put on tennis shoes, coach from 3:30 p.m. to 4:30 p.m. in my shirt and tie and then take off the tennis shoes and come back to the office and work a little later that evening. You can do these things if you try, but you have to make the commitment, because I learned the hard way that your children grow up only once.

I have a wonderful relationship with my granddaughter. She came at a time when we were under tremendous stress as a corporation. We were going through the first three-way utility merger since the early 1930s, and I was living on airplanes and doing road shows. But the stark reality of my first and only grandchild came into my life, and I altered my life right in the middle of all of that chaos. We'd be at the typical meeting at six o'clock, huddled around a table, and I'd say to my male and female colleagues, "Guys, I'm out of here. I'm going to see my granddaughter." I found it liberating.

I find that this is a generational issue. I'm pleased to learn from the younger people who come in and work very hard and contribute tremendously to the corporation. But they make it very clear in a nonoffensive way that they want a life outside of work and that they enjoy life outside of work. I have come to respect that. It may have been a bit grudging at first, but now I fully respect and encourage it.

When I see young people working what I think are inordinately long hours in the name of ambition and getting ahead, I pull them aside and say, "Listen, you have children. They're going to grow up and they're only going to be children once. Go enjoy it."

I'm not sure how much impact I'm having on them, but then again, they're certainly not hearing from their supervisors

the old adage, "Don't work all night but
have it on my desk in the morning." We try
not to do those types of things here. There
are times here—just as everywhere else—
when you're in a crisis mode and you have to
work in a concerted period. But we tend to
tell people after those periods are over to
take some time, relax, recharge the battery;
go reacquaint yourself with your family and
your friends.

If you're looking at work-life balance, I
don't really think you can find a correlation
that says the company is more productive or
more profitable the longer and harder people work. I don't think that's true. You can
find correlations between the quality of life
within a corporation and the productivity
of its employees. It may sound simple,
mundane, or pedestrian, but I believe that
happy employees are more productive
employees than those who are always tired
and dragging.

We encourage an appropriate work-life
balance and wellness in the workplace. We

spend a lot of time and attention on that. We have constructive Web sites to suggest to people that they take care of themselves personally and mentally as well as physically. Certainly, a large part of the mental component is making sure you have appropriate relationships with friends and family.

When we talk about work-life balance, I think I learned that lesson the hard way. I probably have a little guilt that I'm living with, particularly when I spend time with my granddaughter and I ask myself whether I devoted this much time and attention to her mother. Fortunately, she grew up well, and she's a productive, contributing member of society. She's happy, and she's presented me with a great granddaughter, so hopefully I didn't do too much damage in that relationship. But if I had to do it over again, I would spend more time with my children than I did.

TAKEAWAYS

- ⚏ Particularly for ambitious people working their way up, it is challenging to appropriately balance work life with family life, friends, and building relationships.

- ⚏ Happy employees are more productive employees than those who are always tired and dragging.

- ⚏ People need to take care of themselves mentally as well as physically, and a large part of the mental component is having appropriate relationships with friends and family.

Keeping Your Balance

Laura Tyson

National Economic Adviser to
President Bill Clinton

THIS IS A LESSON about the constant
struggle to achieve appropriate balance
in life between work and the rest of life.
It's a struggle that may be particularly
pronounced for women, but I think over
time it has become more and more an issue
that everyone in the workforce deals with.

Loving Your Work

For me, I had had the luxury of an academic profession. And an academic profession does allow you, almost naturally, to have balance. Because when you do your research—in the middle of the night if you want, on weekends, how much research you do in a given year, if you have a child, maybe a little less for a couple of years, a little more a couple of years later—there is a kind of ease of balance. I later realized that balance was a great luxury, because once I arrived in Washington to head the Council of Economic Advisers and was therefore part of the West Wing, part of the White House, I was put in an atmosphere were there was essentially very little attention to the balance issue and very little give in the schedule.

Indeed, the standard that many people see by watching shows like *The West Wing* is that meetings can be called anytime—day or night, weekends—that essentially the West Wing never closes. The president is never not the president. So I had very quickly to grapple with this issue of balance. I had a relatively young child and a husband who

came with me to Washington, who changed
their lives to be with me, to support me in
this job, and felt very much as the spouses
and children of all of the people at that level
felt: that they were doing the jobs along with
the person doing the job. It was a family
job; that is, the family was influenced every
minute by the existence of the demands of
the job.

Once I realized the severity of the trade-
offs, I had to think about how to handle it.
Part of the way I now think about it—and I
learned in that period—is you can't achieve
balance perfectly at every point in your life.
So the big balance issue here is that for some
number of years your life may be out of balance, and then you can offset that some
years later.

I served one full term, four years, with
the Clinton administration. A number of
my colleagues served four years and then
decided to leave. When they decided to
leave, in my case or in the case, for example,
of the Secretary of Labor, who was a very
good friend of mine, our reasons were

balance reasons. Indeed, both Robert
Reich, the Secretary of Labor, and I personally very much wanted to stay, and we
had many opportunities to stay. So this was
not at all a question of not having professional opportunities; they were there. But
after four years, our families, our relationships, everything else in our life other than
having the positions we had was at risk,
underinvested in, and needed some of our
attention.

The personal lessons that come out of
this—in terms of thinking about what an in-
dividual might do in an organization, or
even with their family, for example—would
be, one, to manage expectations. In some
years, and some months, and some period
of time, the expectations for how much time
you actually have are going to be lower than
at other times. Managing expectations
means being realistic; taking away the
misleading statement that you can do it all,
you can have it all, you are some sort of
superhuman being. It's just nonsense. It's
not managing expectations; it's creating

expectations that will be frustrated and not realized.

So, for example, it would have been unreasonable entirely to say I could leave the White House at five o'clock in the afternoon. That was entirely unreasonable. To say I could leave it at eight o'clock at night was actually quite reasonable. I would say, therefore, to both the members of the council that I headed and to my family, I will leave the White House at eight o' clock; that is a reasonable expectation. So both sides don't expect me to leave earlier, but I can manage that. That's managing expectations.

Planning really is—there's a lot of evidence and discussion out there about women's ability to multitask—part of the necessity. If you're juggling a lot of things, you do actually have to have pretty detailed plans. And they can be daily plans such as, "I will, this day, go to a meeting at seven o'clock in the morning, even though I won't be able to drive my son to school." But there are actually more important lifetime plans.

It's a little bit like, "I will be in this location, I will do this for three years, and then I will try to make an adjustment, because my son is going to high school, and I want him to be in a certain place at that point."

So I do think planning is an important part of this, as well as managing expectations.

TAKEAWAYS

- ⧎ Although particularly pronounced for women, the struggle to achieve appropriate balance between work and the rest of life has become an issue that everyone in the workforce deals with.

- ⧎ You can't achieve balance perfectly at every point in your life; for some years, your life may be out of balance, which you can offset some years later.

Keeping Your Balance

🔱 Managing expectations and planning, both daily and over the course of years, are powerful tools for balancing the demands of work with other commitments and activities.

Strive for Perfection

Peggy Fleming

Olympic Figure Skating Gold Medalist;
Co-Owner, Fleming Jenkins
Vineyards & Winery

MY GREATEST LIFE lessons came from
the practice sessions I had with my final
coach, Carlo Fassi, at the Broadmoor. That
was back in the late 1960s, and I was sixteen,
seventeen, eighteen, and nineteen years
old. He always instilled in us to really do

quality practices, not just skate for an hour
and go through the motions. "If you're
going to do that," he said, "just do a shorter
session and leave."

What that instilled in me was to practice
perfection. Every time I skated and had a
lesson from him, I tried to think of a performance. I tried to think of the crowd. I
tried to think of how that pressure would
feel. I actually came up with a game that I
did at every lesson: I would try to do a per-
fect lesson. That made it even more difficult; I didn't want to make one mistake in
the hour I had with this coach. It was fun. I
think he respected that, too; and it was fun
for him to have a student who was giving it
her all at a practice session.

What I learned was that practicing perfection, not cheating yourself, is the best way to
go through life. Even today, when I go for a
run, I have that little voice in my head saying, "I've committed to this hour. I'm going
to keep running the whole time. If I stop,
I'm cheating, and I'm not getting the benefit out of this. I'm only cheating myself."

Strive for Perfection

So I just keep plugging along. When I had my cancer ten years ago, I was going through radiation. My tool for figuring out whether I was OK or not, or whether I was strong or weak, was to continue my normal workouts with my friends. In the beginning, it was a little hard, but by the end—because I kept doing it throughout the whole treatment—I was strong, and I got back to being myself much quicker.

My husband was a physician for more than thirty years, and he strove for perfection every day. We have a career together in the winery, and it's all about perfection as well. We don't want to sell a wine that we don't love. We want to do the best we can and where quality is the most important thing that we do. When I look back on all those practice sessions that I went to and now being in the wine business, I think practicing perfection every day is paying off.

TAKEAWAYS

- ⧗ Imagining as many conditions as possible surrounding your performance at the time you practice increases its effectiveness.

- ⧗ Practicing perfection, not cheating yourself, is the best way to go through life.

- ⧗ Practicing perfection every day pays off.

Step Out of Your Comfort Zone

William Harrison

Former Chairman
JPMorgan Chase & Co.

I GREW UP in a small town in North Carolina. I used to work in my grandfather's bank in the summertime there—he was president of it—and he always told me when I graduated from college, I should go to New York, work a couple of years, and

Loving Your Work

then come back home. When I graduated
from the University of North Carolina in
1967, I really didn't know what I wanted to
do, but I decided that banking was probably
a good pursuit, partly because of my grandfather's advice. So I focused on that, and
I had offers from both a couple of very good
North Carolina banks and a couple of very
good New York banks. Then I had a
dilemma: which one should I take?

My natural inclination was to play into
my comfort zone. My comfort zone, of
course, was North Carolina. That's where I
grew up, that's where I had my friends, and
that's where I'd gone to school. So that was
the easy decision and the decision I wanted
to make, but somehow I convinced myself
that I should get out of that environment,
that I should push myself—only for two
years—go to New York, and I'd probably
be better off for it. I did that, and lo and
behold, I got to New York and I found out
that I loved the job. I loved working every
day, and I loved the environment of

Step Out of Your Comfort Zone

New York. Thirty-eight years later, I'm still here.

I think some of the lessons from that—and I give this advice to all of my colleagues, people who have worked for me now over the years—is that if you want to grow and develop, you have to take risks; you have to push yourself out of your comfort zone. You've got to be thoughtful about it, of course, but you've got to do that. And if you don't do that, you're probably not maximizing your opportunities or your potential.

Here's another thing that played into that, which I try to do with my kids as well. My family would go to Maine in the summertime from North Carolina. It was a long drive; New York was a halfway point, so we'd always stay here. As a kid, I spent a couple of days in New York every summer. I got to be very familiar with it. If it hadn't been for that experience, I don't think that I would have gotten comfortable getting out of my comfort zone in North Carolina and taking this job in New York.

Loving Your Work

So another lesson would be: with colleagues, with friends, with family, give them
different experiences because those experiences enable them to make broader decisions. Experiences make them look at the
world in a different way. When they were
considering a global assignment somewhere
outside of, say, New York or wherever they
were located, I would strongly encourage
them to take it, even though a lot of people
had a first reaction of "I don't really want to
do that. My family is not going to be comfortable; it's going to be hard." I have en-
couraged them to do it, because they will
enhance their career opportunities, they
will enhance their whole outlook on the
world, and their family will end up enjoying
the experience.

Sure, it's tough initially to make change,
but I've used some of my own experiences to
encourage people around the company to
take more risks, to get out of their comfort
zone, whatever it is. I feel very strongly
about that philosophy.

Step Out of Your Comfort Zone

TAKEAWAYS

◄ If you want to grow and develop, you have to take risks and push yourself out of your comfort zone.

◄ If you don't take risks, you're probably not maximizing your opportunities or your potential.

◄ Encourage colleagues, friends, and family to try different experiences, because those experiences will enable them to make broader decisions.

Always Be on the Lookout for Big Ideas

Kay Koplovitz

Founder, USA Networks

I WAS A STUDENT at the University of Wisconsin back in the late 1960s, and I had my mind set on going to medical school. I was a science major in biological sciences. After working many jobs to pay my way through school, I decided I deserved a little

Loving Your Work

bit of vacation. I went off to Europe, mostly to party, I must say, but I also took in some lectures by some people that I thought would be interesting to hear.

I stopped in London and heard somebody that most people know today; they know him for science fiction. He was talking about the theory of geosynchronous orbiting satellites. "Wow," you say. "How sexy is that?" Well, I thought it was really cool, and I began to think about the power of these satellites and how they could communicate with people beyond borders, penetrate despotic governments, and get to the people. I thought this was really, really compelling, and, of course, the man who was talking at the time was Arthur C. Clarke, known for many science fiction novels, but also for writing the theory of geosynchronous orbiting satellites, coming out of the Second World War. So this was a gentleman who really turned my head, because I liked science. I was in biological science, but all of a sudden I'm in satellite technology and looking to do something else.

Be on the Lookout for Big Ideas

The idea of being able to use these tools to communicate to any point on earth from satellites that appeared to be geosynchronous above that point on earth—with signals traveling around the earth unabated—I thought was so powerful. It captivated me. I mean, I literally walked out of the lecture hall thinking to myself, "I've got to do something about this." I think it's that passion. He was so passionate about the subject, and his passion grabbed me. It just grabbed me, and it started me thinking about what could be done. I was quite determined to study geosynchronous orbiting satellites, study governments, and understand how you could penetrate beyond those government borders to really talk to people, breach those borders with messages that perhaps people hadn't heard before.

I went back and finished school, and wrote my master's thesis on satellites, geosynchronous orbiting satellites, and what they could do for communications processes, how they could bring people together at very different points on earth.

Loving Your Work

I thought that was really, really compelling
to opening up news, information, and entertainment to be shared among people of
the world and bring people closer together.
Of course, I was thinking of something that
was a little bit more altruistic at the time,
but today we really expect to have anything—
all the news, all the sports, everything—all
the time and everywhere. It's a result of
bringing these satellites into the mainstream
in business.

So what did I learn from this process?
I learned, keep your mind open for ideas.
You might find a really big one someday.
I did. This one changed the course of my
direction in life. I've loved every minute of
it, and I think it's because I owned the idea.
I took it as my own passion, and I owned it.
And when you own an idea, you have the
opportunity to really bring other people
along with you.

TAKEAWAYS

- Keep your mind open for ideas, because you might find a really big one that could change the course of your direction in life.

- When you own an idea, you have the opportunity to bring other people along with you.

———◆◆◆———

Focus on Retaining Talent, Not Hiring

———◆◆◆———

Cali Ressler and Jody Thompson

Founders, CultureRx

Jody Thompson: Companies today are looking to figure out how to hire the right talent. In our experience, if you shift your focus to retaining the talent you have and look at people who potentially aren't doing the work and let them go work somewhere else, you're actually creating an environment where you'll retain people instead of figuring out how to get them back once they've left.

When we talk about retaining people and creating the right kind of work environment, one of the things companies are going to tackle in the future is, what do we do with those crazy Gen Ys—that next generation, that completely untethered generation of people who are not connected to anything but their device, who are connected all over the world with their device, who have Facebook and all sorts of ways to collaborate and communicate? Because what we do is, we bring them into an environment that's completely tethered: desktop computer, a cube, meeting face-to-face with people all the time, and a manager who's managing by walking around.

Creating an environment to retain the talent that's coming is what's going to be important in the future. I'm going to paint the picture of a Gen Y person in a tethered, traditional organization:

On Sunday night, I am completely dreading the week ahead of me. I know it's coming; it starts at eight o'clock Monday morning. All week I have no control over my time or what I do, because now the company has control over that. So I get up in the morning, I'm rushing around, and I have to quickly get out in rush-hour traffic because if I'm not in my cube at eight o'clock, then I get that look: "Gee, bankers' hours again today. I was here; why weren't you here?"

So I do some work. I'm in my cube, and now I get interrupted. I try to get something done, and I get interrupted again. All day long, I'm struggling to do my work. And I'm also thinking about all the other things I have to do in my life, so I surf the Internet for a while and my boss walks by. I quickly put the monitor to a different direction so they don't see it. And all day long, I'm struggling, struggling, struggling because I don't have any control over my time.

Cali Ressler: That was Mark the first three weeks that he worked in the company, before he was in a results-only work environment. Here's what he looks like

Loving Your Work

now: Mark is someone who has complete control over how he spends his time every single day. Sometimes he decides, "I'm going to work really hard for two weeks and then have the next two weeks where I am traveling the country, following my favorite rock band." Sometimes Mark is someone who sleeps in until eleven o'clock on a Tuesday before he calls in for a meeting, then does some grocery shopping, and comes back and does some e-mails.

Mark has told us he does not own an alarm clock anymore. In corporate America, you don't hear that very often. He doesn't have an alarm clock; he lets the sun wake him up. He is someone who can do his work while he's watching ESPN, watching his favorite game. He goes to the mountains to do some hiking, and we know that for him that is a place that gives him the spark to do his work. And today he is someone who can find that spark wherever he needs to find it, whenever he needs to find it, and that's what's made this kind of environment priceless for him.

Focus on Retaining Talent

Jody Thompson: Here's the paradigm shift for managers. If I have an employee who's sitting in a tent on a mountain, does that look like work? If my employee is sitting in a coffee shop, does that look like work? If my employee is sitting at the beach, does that look like work? So what we're shifting in a manager's mind is, what looks like work might not really be work.

If you think about your employees sitting in cubes all day, you have a false sense that they're working. You think that they're working because it looks like work—they're in the office building; they're in the cube; they have a computer in front of them; they're talking to the people around them. That looks like work. And as a manager, I feel uncomfortable if I allow my people to work in other places, because I wonder if I'm not getting the hours out of them. I wonder if they're not working.

But managers in a results-only work environment look at results only—not where people are working, not what time they're working, but that they're getting the work

done. That's the real shift for managers:
I don't own your time anymore; I own
making clear your goals and expectations.

Cali Ressler: And Mark's manager is extremely clear about goals and expectations, and Mark understands those, which is why Mark's productivity has now increased four times since he migrated to a results-only work environment. He would never go to another company.

We've asked him, "How much would [another] company have to pay you to leave?"

And he says to us, "They couldn't pay me enough money. I will never leave this. Why would I leave this job that allows me to live exactly how I've always wanted to live?"

—•—

TAKEAWAYS

—•—

⊱ Creating an environment to retain the talent that's coming is what's going to be important in the future.

Focus on Retaining Talent

⚏ Employees may give every appearance
of working, yet not be working, just as
employees may give every appearance
of not working, yet be working.

⚏ Managers in a results-only work
environment look only at results, not
the hours and locations where
employees produce them.

—◆◆◆—

The Way We Work

—◆◆◆—

Sir David Bell

Director for People, Pearson

THE PEOPLE WHO come to work don't
just exist inside their organizations; they
have other lives and are fully rounded
people. If a business forgets that, then it
does so at its peril.

One of the very important things we
strive to do is understand a little bit about
work-life balance, as some people call it,
not in a soft way, but because it is a good
investment. If you bother to understand the

issues confronting people, then they will work better and so will the company. In the end, their commitment is going to deepen.

If you look at this company fifty years ago, we've come a long way. In fact, I met a very old woman the other day who was secretary to Lord Cowdray, a Pearson chairman, years ago. She remembered that one man with a child had asked, "Could I take off Boxing Day as well as Christmas Day?" His boss had said, "Why would you want that? You can have Christmas Day off, but you can't have the day after." She thought that was fine, so in terms of corporate culture, we've come a long way.

When I started as the advertisement director of the *Financial Times*, we employed no women in senior jobs at all. I promoted a lot of women, but as I was doing this, I heard one day that a woman who was a mother had asked if she could go home to look after one of her children who was ill. The man for whom she worked said, "No, you came here to work, and you can wait until the end of the day."

The Way We Work

I had them all in, and I said that if that ever happened again, whoever it was who said no would be fired. I think they were astonished by this, but it never happened again. Most of the men in that room were only there because they had partners at home who were looking after their children for them. Once you accept that that's the balance, the idea of balancing it better becomes easier.

You have to assume that the people who work for you are not trying to slide out and stop working; they're not making excuses. It is very rare for somebody to say, "I've got to go home to look after my child," and for it to be dishonest. It's very unusual. We start with the assumption that it is completely honest. If somebody says that, we believe them. If that's the case, they will be much more effective if they are at home and have dealt with this problem, than if they are sitting at their desk worrying about it.

We have more women than men working for us, and this has forced us to think more about this. But that isn't the only reason; it is just a question of equity and fundamental fairness.

We are never going to have a situation where people will be working from home all the time. We don't believe this idea that people can be in a creative business and do everything from home is going to work. We may find that people work at home for a greater proportion of their time than they currently do, but we actually find that bringing people together, the creativity of the spark, is very important.

I think we're going to be more flexible about the school holidays, where sometimes people need to be at home more. We are going to start thinking about people working a number of hours across a whole year rather than across a week or a month. So we are going to be more balanced and flexible.

TAKEAWAYS

- People who come to work don't just exist inside their organizations; they have other lives and are fully rounded people.

- It is in a business's best interests to appreciate that its employees have full lives outside of work.

- If you bother to understand the issues confronting people, their commitment to the company will deepen; they will work better, and so will the company.

⊰ ABOUT THE ⊱ CONTRIBUTORS

Sir David Bell is a Director of Pearson, an international media company. He is also Chairman of the Financial Times Group, having been Chief Executive of the *Financial Times* since 1993.

In July 1998, Sir David was appointed Pearson's Director for People with responsibility for the recruitment, motivation, development, and reward of employees across the Pearson Group. In addition, he is a Director of *The Economist*, the Vitec Group plc, and The Windmill Partnership.

Sir David is Chairman of the following organizations: Common Purpose International, Crisis, Sadler's Wells, and the International Youth Foundation.

He was also Chairman of the Millennium Bridge Trust (1995–2000), which was responsible for conceiving the first new bridge across the Thames in one hundred years.

Sir David was educated at Cambridge University and the University of Pennsylvania.

Warren Bennis is University Professor and Distinguished Professor of Business Administration and Founding Chairman of the Leadership

About the Contributors

Institute at the Marshall School of Business, University of Southern California.

Professor Bennis has served on the faculty of the MIT Sloan School of Management, where he was Chairman of the Organizational Studies Department. He is a former faculty member of Harvard University and Boston University, and former Provost and Executive Vice President of State University of New York at Buffalo. He was President of the University of Cincinnati from 1971 to 1977.

Professor Bennis is also Chairman of the Advisory Board of the Center for Public Leadership at Harvard's Kennedy School. He has written more than two dozen books and many articles on leadership, change, and creative collaboration. He is a consultant for *Fortune* 500 companies and has served as an adviser to four U.S. presidents.

His book *Leaders* was recently cited by the *Financial Times* as one of the top fifty business books of all times. *An Invented Life: Reflections on Leadership and Change* was nominated for a Pulitzer. His other books include *Geeks & Geezers*, *Organizing Genius*, and *Managing the Dream*.

Professor Bennis served in the U.S. Army between 1943 and 1947; he was one of the youngest infantry commanders in the European theater of operations and was awarded the Purple Heart and Bronze Star.

Amy Butte is the former CFO of MF Group, a leading broker of exchange-listed futures and options.

About the Contributors

Ms. Butte started her career in equity research at Merrill Lynch and also worked at Bridge Trading Company, Merrin Financial, and Andersen Consulting. She then moved to Bear Stearns & Co., where she became a Senior Managing Director in equity research, responsible for coverage of the brokerage, asset-gathering, and financial technology industries.

Following this, Ms. Butte became Chief Strategist and CFO with Credit Suisse First Boston's financial services division. There she helped lead the development of the firm's global asset-gathering division and the sale of the firm's correspondent clearing business, Pershing, to the Bank of New York.

Ms. Butte joined the New York Stock Exchange in February 2004 as Executive Vice President and became CFO two months later. In this role, she was responsible for all NYSE financial planning and operations. Ms. Butte stepped down as CFO in late 2006.

Ms. Butte joined Man Financial in August 2006 as CFO. In 2007, she became CFO and Director of MF Group, which formed when Man Financial spun off its brokerage unit. She stepped down from MF Group in 2008.

Ms. Butte is Co-Chairman of the New York City Ballet's Corporate Advisory Board and is an active member of the New York Women's Foundation.

Maxine Clark is the Chairman and Chief Executive Bear for Build-A-Bear Workshop, Inc., an interactive, make-your-own stuffed animal, retail-entertainment experience.

From November 1992 until January 1996, Ms. Clark was the President of Payless ShoeSource, Inc., a leading footwear retailer. Prior to joining Payless, Ms. Clark spent more than nineteen years in various divisions of the May Department Stores Company in areas including merchandise development, planning, and research; marketing; and product development.

In 1997, she founded Build-A-Bear Workshop and has served as its Chief Executive Bear from the beginning. She served as President from 1997 to 2004 and became Chairman in April 2000.

Ms. Clark is a Director of the J.C. Penney Company, Inc. She also serves on the boards of the International Council of Shopping Centers and Washington University in St. Louis, and is a Director of BJC Healthcare, a nonprofit healthcare organization.

Erroll Davis Jr. is the former Chairman of Alliant Energy Corporation. Currently, he is the Chancellor of the University System of Georgia.

Mr. Davis worked in the energy industry for more than twenty-five years. He joined Wisconsin Power and Light Company in 1978, became CEO ten years later, and also served as President until 1998. Following the merger of Wisconsin Power and Light with Alliant Energy in 1998, Mr. Davis became President and CEO of Alliant Energy.

He stayed in the role of CEO until June 2005 and remained as Chairman of the company until 2006, when he stepped down. Mr. Davis also served as CEO of Alliant Energy Resources, Inc., and Iowa Power and Light Co. (or their predecessor companies) following the merger.

In February 2006, Mr. Davis took office as Chancellor of the University System of Georgia, where he is responsible for the state's thirty-five public colleges and universities; approximately 283,000 students; 40,000 faculty and staff; and an annual budget of $6.1 billion. The University System also has administrative responsibility for the Georgia Public Library Service, which manages the state's fifty-eight public library systems.

Mr. Davis is a member of the board of directors of General Motors, BP plc, and Union Pacific Corp., and serves on the National Commission on Energy Policy. He is a member of numerous professional associations and civic organizations and a former member of the U.S. Olympic Committee Board (2004–2008).

Peggy Fleming is a three-time World Figure Skating Champion and an Olympic figure skating gold medalist.

She is also co-owner with her husband, Dr. Greg Jenkins, of Fleming Jenkins Vineyards & Winery. The winery was begun in 1999 with a small chardonnay vineyard in the foothills of the Santa Cruz Mountains of California. Today, they farm and harvest the vineyard, making new wines in the historic Novitiate Winery.

Ms. Fleming is a native of California, where as a child she was inspired to take up figure skating. An early success, she garnered five U.S. titles, three world titles, and in 1968 won an Olympic gold medal in Grenoble, France. During her travels, Coach Carlo Fassi introduced her to the customs, cultures, and most importantly, the cuisine of the countries she visited.

Skating on television led to appearances on programs ranging from *Diagnosis Murder* and *Newhart* to hosting a special on poaching in East Africa and also commercial endorsements. Since 1981, Ms. Fleming's career as an on-air analyst for ABC Sports has taken her to national, world, and Olympic competitions. The diversity of Ms. Fleming's marketing development set the standard for today's generation of figure skaters.

Ms. Fleming has served on several community project boards, such as San Jose's Sports Authority, and as Honorary Chairman for Easter Seals and the PTA. She was also the National Spokesperson for the National Osteoporosis Foundation. She has been invited to the White House by four different administrations and is a frequently sought-after speaker.

William Harrison was the Chairman and CEO of JPMorgan Chase & Co. from November 2001 to December 2005. He was Chairman from

About the Contributors

December 2005 until his retirement in December 2006.

Between January and November 2001, he held the position of President and CEO. Prior to the merger with J.P. Morgan, Mr. Harrison was Chairman and CEO of the Chase Manhattan Corporation, a position he assumed in January 2000.

He held the same responsibilities at Chemical Bank prior to its merger with Chase in 1996. In 1978, he moved to London to take responsibility for the bank's U.K. business, and in 1982, was promoted to division head of Europe. Mr. Harrison returned to the United States in 1983 to run the U.S. corporate division and was put in charge of the bank's global banking and corporate finance group three years later.

Mr. Harrison is a Director for Cousins Properties, Inc., and has been a Director for Merck & Co. since 1999.

Kay Koplovitz is the Founder of USA Networks.

She is also the Founder and CEO of Koplovitz & Co., a media advisory and investment firm, and is widely acclaimed as a leader in the U.S. television and emerging media businesses, a successful entrepreneur, seasoned venture capitalist, and author.

Ms. Koplovitz became the first woman network president in television history when she founded USA Networks in 1977 under the banner of Madison Square Garden Sports. It was the first advertising-supported basic cable network.

About the Contributors

A visionary of sports television, Ms. Koplovitz launched major professional and collegiate sports on cable television by negotiating the first contracts for Major League Baseball, the National Basketball Association, and the National Hockey League.

In 1992, Ms. Koplovitz was instrumental in the launch of the Sci-Fi Channel. Two years later, she introduced USA Networks International. She subsequently started Springboard, a nonprofit forum to connect women with venture capital. She currently serves as Springboard's Chairman.

In 1998, President Clinton appointed Ms. Koplovitz as Chair of the bipartisan National Women's Business Council. In 2001, Ms. Koplovitz cofounded Boldcap Ventures, a venture fund backed exclusively by high-net-worth women seeking to grow their portfolios with venture investments.

Ms. Koplovitz is also Chairman of Liz Claiborne, having joined the board as a Director in 1992. She serves on the boards of a number of nonprofit organizations, including the Central Park Conservancy and the Museum of Television and Radio. She is the author of *Big Women, Big Ideas*, published in May 2002.

Howard Lester is the Chairman and CEO of Williams-Sonoma, a premier specialty retailer of home furnishings and cooking supplies and equipment.

Mr. Lester has extensive experience in computer operations and spent fifteen years in the computer

About the Contributors

industry before entering retailing. After six years with Computer Sciences Corporation, he became Executive Vice President of Bradford National Corporation, which acquired Centurex.

Mr. Lester purchased Williams-Sonoma in 1978, and since then he has held the positions of President, CEO, and Chairman.

Mr. Lester is also on the Executive Council of University of California, San Francisco. He is on the advisory boards of the Retail Management Institute of Santa Clara University and the Walter A. Haas School of Business at the University of California, Berkeley.

He previously served on the boards of the Boy Scouts of America; Conner Peripherals, Inc.; Harold's Stores, Inc.; and the International Association of Shopping Centers.

Stacy Peralta is a former professional skateboarder and the award-winning director of the documentary, *Dogtown and Z-Boys*.

Mr. Peralta is also a director for the film company Nonfiction Unlimited. The company was founded in 1995 as the advertising agency Nonfiction Spots. Nonfiction Unlimited now creates compelling documentaries as well as brand campaigns, commercials, and episodic series for television and the Internet. Clients have included Adidas, Anheuser-Busch, BP, Coca-Cola, Columbia Sportswear, Dove, Ford, Hitachi, Intel, MasterCard, Nike, Nokia, Sprint, Target, the U.S. Army, the U.S. Navy, Vans, Verizon, and Visa.

About the Contributors

Mr. Peralta grew up in West Los Angeles, California, on the beaches of Venice and Santa Monica. A founder of the 1970s skateboard movement, Mr. Peralta was one of the first skaters to win product endorsements and television and film appearances. At the age of nineteen, Mr. Peralta was the highest-ranked professional skateboarder in America.

Soon after, he joined with manufacturer George Powell to form the Powell-Peralta skate-gear company. With the financial backing of Powell-Peralta, Peralta formed the Bones Brigade, a skate team composed of some best skaters at the time, many of whom revolutionized modern skateboarding. He also began directing and producing the first skating demo videos in an eight-part series known as *The Bones Brigade Video Show*.

In 1992, Mr. Peralta left the company he founded with Powell to direct and produce for television full time. He found television somewhat tame and soon struck out on his own. Teaching himself how to use a camera, he quickly found his niche. His groundbreaking documentary *Dogtown and Z-Boys* was based on his own skating days. The film won a Sundance Award in 2001 and was the basis for the 2005 dramatic film *Lords of Dogtown*.

Mr. Peralta's sports expertise came to the fore again in *Riding Giants*, a documentary about big-wave surfing. His skills as both an entrepreneur and skate demo filmmaker went into his work on the video

game, *Tony Hawk's Underground*, in which
Mr. Peralta plays himself.

Cali Ressler and **Jody Thompson** are the co-
founders of CultureRx, a wholly owned subsidiary
of Best Buy Co., Inc., a specialty retailer of consumer electronics, personal computers, entertainment software, and appliances.

Ms. Ressler was a manager of Best Buy's work-
life balance program when she started the ROWE
(results-only work environment) experiment at a
division in Minneapolis. Ms. Thompson was Best
Buy's organizational guru when she learned of the
experiment. Together they worked to implement
ROWE as a companywide program. Ms. Thompson
and Ms. Ressler then founded CultureRx, a consulting company specializing in ROWE.

Ms. Ressler and Ms. Thompson are the coau-
thors of the book *Why Work Sucks and How to Fix It*. They
have been featured in *BusinessWeek, HR Magazine*, the
New York Times, and *Time*, and on *60 Minutes* and
National Public Radio.

Jerry Rice is a former wide receiver for the San
Francisco 49ers. He is considered to be the greatest
wide receiver in the history of the National Football
League, holding records for nearly every career
receiving category.

After excelling in high school football, Mr. Rice
attended Mississippi Valley State University, where
he had a total of fifty-one touchdown catches. In

About the Contributors

1984, he was named an AP All-American and finished ninth in the Heisman Trophy balloting.

In 1985, Mr. Rice began his rookie season as a first-round draft pick for the 49ers. That season, he had 49 catches for 927 yards, and the following season, he had 86 catches for 1,570 yards. This was the first of six seasons when he led the NFL in receiving and touchdown receptions.

In the 1988 postseason, he was instrumental in the 49ers' win in both the National Football Conference title game and Super Bowl XXIII. For his performance, he became only the third wide receiver ever to win Super Bowl MVP honors. In 1989, he helped the team achieve another Super Bowl win when he made a record three touchdown receptions. The 49ers won yet another Super Bowl victory in 1994. In 1995, Mr. Rice broke the NFL record for most receiving yards in a single season.

In 2001, Mr. Rice began playing for the Oakland Raiders and became the only player in NFL history to achieve twenty thousand career receiving yards. In 2004, he played for the Seattle Seahawks, where he played his three hundredth career game. Mr. Rice joined the Denver Broncos in 2005, but he retired shortly before the season began.

Peter Seligmann is the Cofounder, Chairman, and CEO of Conservation International, an organization that creates lasting solutions to biodiversity and conserves the earth's living heritage.

About the Contributors

Mr. Seligmann received his master's degree from the Yale School of Forestry in 1974, and soon after, he began a job in conservation. During a visit to Peru, he was struck by the contrast between the country's enormous biological wealth and its staggering poverty. In 1987, he cofounded Conservation International, based on a vision that people could live peacefully with nature. Since then, the organization has grown to forty-five field offices on four continents.

In 1998, Conservation International established the Center for Applied Biodiversity Science and, in 2001, the Center for Environmental Leadership in Business. In 2000, Conservation International launched the Critical Ecosystem Partnership Fund in collaboration with the World Bank and the John D. and Catherine T. MacArthur Foundation.

In 2001, Mr. Seligmann was awarded the Netherlands' Order of the Golden Ark. He serves on the board of the Wild Salmon Center in Portland, Oregon, and the advisory councils of the Jackson Hole Land Trust, Ecotrust, and other nonprofit organizations, including the Keidanren Nature Conservation Fund. In 2000, President Clinton named him a member of the Enterprise for the Americas board.

Laura Tyson is currently a Professor at the University of California, Berkeley. Prior to returning for her second stint at the University of California, Professor Tyson was the Dean of the London

About the Contributors

Business School and former White House National Economic Adviser.

Professor Tyson became Dean of the London Business School in 2002 and left that position at the end of 2006. Previously, she had been Dean of the Haas School of Business at the University of California, Berkeley, and, before that, Professor of Economics and Business Administration at the University of California.

Professor Tyson served in the Clinton administration from January 1993 to December 1996. Between February 1995 and December 1996, she served as the President's National Economic Adviser and was the highest-ranking woman in the Clinton White House.

Professor Tyson was a key architect of President Clinton's domestic and international policy agenda during his first term in office. As the administration's top economic adviser, she managed all economic policy making throughout the executive branch.

Prior to this appointment, she served as the sixteenth Chairman of the White House Council of Economic Advisers, the first woman to hold that post. Before joining the Clinton administration, Professor Tyson published a number of books and articles on industrial competitiveness and trade, including *Who's Bashing Whom? Trade Conflict in High-Technology Industries*.

Professor Tyson has served on three boards of directors since 1997: Morgan Stanley, Eastman Kodak, and AT&T (formerly Ameritech Corp.).

⊰ ACKNOWLEDGMENTS ⊱

First and foremost, a heartfelt thanks goes to all the executives who have candidly shared their hard-won experience and battle-tested insights for the *Lessons Learned* series.

We would also like to thank Condé Nast Portfolio for permission to use lessons produced in partnership as part of an online feature series, "Back to Back: Winning Second Acts." For more Portfolio and Condé Nast offerings, visit www.portfolio.com.

Angelia Herrin at Harvard Business Publishing consistently offered unwavering support, good humor, and counsel from the inception of this ambitious project.

Kathleen Carr, Brian Surette, and David Goehring provided invaluable editorial direction, perspective, and encouragement, particularly for this second series. Many thanks to the entire HBP team of designers, copy editors, and marketing professionals who helped bring this series to life.

Much appreciation goes to Jennifer Lynn and Christopher Benoît for research and diligent attention to detail, and to Roberto de Vicq de Cumptich for his imaginative cover designs.

Finally, thanks to James MacKinnon and the entire 50 Lessons team for their time, effort, and steadfast support of this project.

THE LAST PAGE IS
ONLY THE BEGINNING

Watch Free *Lessons Learned*
Video Interviews and Get Additional Resources

You've just read first-hand accounts from the business
world's top leaders, but the learning doesn't have to
end there. 50 Lessons gives you access to:

**Exclusive videos featuring the leaders
profiled in this book**

**Practical advice for putting their
insights into action**

**Challenging questions that
extend your learning**

FREE ONLINE AT:
www.50lessons.com/work